MW01143977

What God Thinks About Psychology

What God Thinks About Psychology

7 spiritual nuggets for making your spiritual journey a practical reality

Rolando Hyman

To order additional copies of this book, contact:
Xlibris
844-714-8691
www.Xlibris.com
Orders@Xlibris.com
828123

Dedication

I would like to dedicate this paperback to my four children and wife Alanna who continues to be a strong support as I engage in writing this epilogue. I would also like to acknowledge the gift of wisdom and knowledge that was given to me by the creator to write about the possibility of a connection between spirituality and psychology. It is my hope that all who read the contents of this book will receive some insight from the arguments that are presented. Hope you have fun as you go on this journey.

Introduction

Spirituality has evolved into several different shapes and forms according to the individual's or organization's interpretation or preference of what works best. There is both denial and acceptance of the possibility of a connection between spirituality and psychology. We will attempt to take the readers of this paperback on a journey that explores if there are any psychological implications of Spirituality. Each point will be supported by biblical text and research evidence from the field of psychotherapy. The intent will be to engage your mind in a somewhat thought-provoking question, does God care about psychology? For those who do not care much about the God factor, this question might not even mean much to you so no pressure. But let us just say for argument's sake God does exist, could God be the originator of psychology? This book will attempt to answer these questions. The questions will be illustrated with stories from real characters, personal experiences, and biblical spiritual psychological text that will give a contextual contemporary perspective on the relationship between spirituality and psychology.

One of the most complex disciplines that are in the professional realm is the field of psychology. This field seeks to study the physiological, emotional, psychological, social, cultural, spiritual, and intergenerational perspectives. Several individuals are missing out on the possibility that there may be a close association of the spiritual and psychological that is ignored or disowned by many professionals. Many attempts to integrate spirituality into their approach to psychology and adapt a counterfeit form of spirituality that is grounded in spiritism can be misleading. The interpretation and acceptance of spirituality that is rooted in the origin of a higher power, or God the creator is often slighted as valuable. We are living in an age of reason and many bright minds are presenting several arguments about neuroscience and how the brain works. There is research on the cognitive implications of psychological disorders. We have those who are eye movement desensitization and reprocessing (EMDR). We have behavioral specialists and psychiatrists who are all recognized as experts in their fields. As I sit here in reflection, I would like to pose my first question here to all these experts, doctors, psychologists, scientists, and physicists. Where did this wisdom come from that is the source of all this learning? There is a text in the Bible that I read some time ago that was quite direct in the way it spoke about wisdom.

The fear of the Lord is the beginning of knowledge, but fools hate wisdom and instruction. **(Proverbs 1:7)**

Would it be fair to say that knowledge and wisdom are similar in meaning? If this is so, then all the so-called scholars whether they accept the existence of God or not are utilizing a gift that has nothing to do with their "brilliance" in their field of expertise but with a gift that they inherited from a creator whose existence they deny wholeheartedly. Now is this an irony or was this a typographical error in the translation of the text? Psychology is considered a science because of all the different facets of human behaviors and functionality. Spirituality could also be considered a science. My reason for this conclusion is because of the complexities that are major elements of spirituality several individuals are closed off. Imagine you were called into a meeting by the chief executive officer (CEO) of your company and he told you to do something unheard of in your field of expertise. Following this direction would make you the laughingstock in the company but doing it is not optional. The decision would label you as delusional, unstable, and maybe even unfit for duty. Following this direction could place you on the unemployment list and could even make you unemployable. There is a similar story about a man named Joshua who was given an assignment by God to go to a city that was very secure and had what was like a retainer wall that went around the city. This wall was wide enough to have two lanes of vehicular traffic running in opposite directions. The citizens who lived within the walls of this city had a false sense of security because their faith was not in anything outside of their political power, the strength of their army, and the weapons that they possessed. The odds were not in favor of Joshua and many who were associated with Joshua might have

3

questioned the validity of this directive that Joshua said he got from God. Let us look at the specific instructions here.

> Then the Lord said to Joshua, "See, I have delivered Jericho into your hands, along with its king and its fighting men. March around the city once with all the armed men. Do this for six days. Have seven priests carry trumpets of rams' horns in front of the ark. On the seventh day, march around the city seven times, with the priests blowing the trumpets. When you hear them sound a long blast on the trumpets, have the whole army give a loud shout; then the wall of the city will collapse and the army will go up, everyone straight in." ….. When the trumpets sounded, the army shouted, and at the sound of the trumpet, when the men gave a loud shout, the wall collapsed; so, everyone charged straight in, and they took the city. (Joshua 6: 2-5 & 20)

Can you imagine what that experience was like for Joshua and how he might have experienced some psychological, and emotional discomfort as he tried to wrap his mind around the task at hand? He had an army but compared to the one he was going against they were outnumbered outgunned and unprepared to make any impact on the city unless something unforeseen happened. The irony of this story is that it was already inevitable that the city was going to be conquered by Joshua, but God still asked him to participate in an act that was never seen before. The strategy that he was asked to use was not like any that was ever seen especially by the army that lived inside the city. The instruction was for them to march around the city. Once every day for six days and then seven times on the seventh day, then let the pastors or priest blow the trumpets, let the army shout at the end, and leave the rest up to me, was what God told Joshua to do. Well, he did as he was told, and as promised the walls of the city were broken into pieces as if they were hit with a giant size sledgehammer and the city was taken over by Joshua and his army. Spiritually this would not make sense to a person who has no belief in a God they have never seen or have no need to believe in. In the realm of psychology, it is much more comforting to know that you have control over the situation, it gives more reassurance. In this scenario, it made no logical sense because unless you were aware of a God of impossibility then this is a weird request, especially if you heard it second hand. On the other hand, this would cause extreme anxiety for many persons who like to have things planned and be in control of the activities that lead up to the finality. This went against all the reasoning of spirituality and psychology but the treatment plan for the success of this "crisis" was already complete.

Spiritual growth and accomplishing positive results will be challenging because it is in many scenarios the most complicated and less favored. In my role as a psychotherapist, I have engaged in conversations with a huge percentage of individuals who are not open or aware of the interrelation between spirituality and psychology and they are searching for meaning and satisfaction that sometimes seem to be always one step ahead because they are resistant to acknowledge the existence of spirituality or even recognize that they are spiritual beings. So, what then is spirituality is what I would like to discuss next to try and bring some clarity to this topic. On the one hand for many people when they hear the word spirituality they think of a force or a focus on a higher power. In some cultures, spirituality is having a connection with a being who possesses supernatural powers. In another context when the word spirituality alludes to it means God and angels and miracles and the sacrifice of His son Jesus. Depending on whom you are communicating with and what their worldview is the expression or understanding of spirituality is oftentimes based on personal preference, cultural norms, and religious and nonreligious based practices that are paraded in different settings across our planet.

So now let us consider this for the next few minutes, most of you expect a society where if not met you feel violated and betrayed. There is an innate volition that is inside of you that arrest your attention and causes a disequilibrium in your psychological and emotional well-being that appeals to healing, recovery, and restoration. Could it be that you have an internal moral thermometer that measures your daily activities and associations and when the atmosphere changes without thinking too long or hard you recognize that you've been violated and immediately you start seeking vindication, justice, and healing from the event? Maybe your moral thermometer is rooted in spirituality. If this is true for all human beings, then you are more spiritual than you are willing to acknowledge. Without knowledge or acceptance of the possibility that you have a percentage of spirituality that is innate and is not determined by your acceptance or refusal it just is. If someone takes something that does not belong to them, you call it dishonesty, stealing, misrepresentation, or an unlawful act. If your partner went out and looked for emotional or sexual satisfaction outside of the relationship you would say it is cheating, betrayal of trust, or grounds for separation or divorce. So, this leaves one to wonder who came up with these ideas and how or why human beings hurt so deeply when these and other forms of activities cause these discomforts that explode deep within your soul and mind. Psychologically you move from being confident and driven and resort to self-doubt and depressive symptoms which leads to self-isolation. Where did all of this begin at the core of who you are as an individual, at the foundations of your psychospiritual being? I would now like to direct your attention to this biblical reference.

And God spoke all these words:
I am the Lord your God, who brought you out of Egypt, out of the land of slavery.
You shall have no other gods before me.
You shall not make for yourself an image in the form of anything in heaven above or on the earth beneath or in the waters below. You shall not bow down to them or worship them; for I, the Lord your God, am a jealous God, punishing the children for the sin of the parents to the third and fourth generation of those who hate me, but showing love to a thousand generations of those who love me and keep my commandments.
You shall not misuse the name of the Lord your God, for the Lord will not hold anyone guiltless who misuses his name.
"Remember the Sabbath day by keeping it holy. Six days you shall labor and do all your work, but the seventh day is a sabbath to the Lord your God. On it you shall not do any work, neither

you, nor your son or daughter, nor your male or female servant, nor your animals, nor any foreigner residing in your towns. For in six days, the Lord made the heavens and the earth, the sea, and all that is in them, but he rested on the seventh day. Therefore, the Lord blessed the Sabbath day and made it holy.

"Honor your father and your mother, so that you may live long in the land the Lord your God is giving you.

You shall not murder.

You shall not commit adultery.

You shall not steal.

You shall not give false testimony against your neighbor.

You shall not covet your neighbor's house. You shall not covet your neighbor's wife, or his male or female servant, his ox or donkey, or anything that belongs to your neighbor." (Exodus 20: 1-17).

The principles that are outlined in this biblical reference appear to be connected to the laws that you practice every day in your personal and professional life. Organizations and individuals depend on ethical conduct that facilitates best practices and promotes stability and good conduct. Whenever there are no rules or modus operandi there is chaos, heartbreak, lawsuits, and psychological malfunctioning. The truth of the matter is that you can ignore the interconnection with spirituality and psychology and disregard the possibility that maybe there is a relationship. The community in which you live is affected by several injustices and the main cry from differing organizations is for there to be less discrimination and more fair play across the board. The Black Lives Matter initiative, the appeal to stop sexual harassment in the workplace, and stop bullying in schools appear to be connected to some form of morality that is a part of your DNA and mine. When you see it or experience it there is something inside you that sends off an alarm that says this is not right. This feeling inside of you sometimes leads to extreme measures like peaceful demonstrations and riots because of the psychological impact this disregard of fairness, equality, and violation of individuation causes on individuals in the community. Could this be because there is a connection between the spiritual and psychological that flips a switch in your psyche?

By nature, you are advocates for fairness and inclusion, and several well-known organizations and individuals lobby for a level playing field for all people. This is sufficient evidence to support the theory that there are some things that you are born with, and it is almost as if it is innate. You and I are part of a system that is intertwined in an inseparable relationship shared between two of the higher sciences namely spirituality and psychology. A relationship with your parents, siblings, and neighbors is important to most persons in society while for others this does not matter but the void that is there is exposed in a display of self-centeredness and socially awkward individuals who are often in denial about the psychological impact this has on their relationships.

Let us now make a Segway to another example that shows a psychological spiritual connection. I am hoping that this next bible reference will make sense to you as you continue your journey in this epilogue.

For as he thinks in his heart, so is he (Proverbs 23:7).

The heart here is referring to the mind and the things that are nurtured in your mind will be displayed in your personality and character. Mental health is a multi-billion-dollar industry that is booming and keeps getting more expensive each year in our community. The Canadian Mental Health Association (CHMA) of British Columbia earmarked a total of $2 billion that is just for mental health and addiction care. This is only one out of the ten provinces in Canada and three territories. We did not include the budget for other countries around the world and mention those countries that do not have the available funding to have a budget for mental health and addiction support. (Canadian Mental Health Association (CMHA), 2020).

The problem of mental health is an issue that continuously steers you in the face for more reasons than one. Many individuals are unaware and unaccepting of the reality that no one is immune to being a candidate for a mental health diagnosis. Whether you struggle with anxiety, depression, low self-esteem, or any other known disorder that is identified in the Diagnostic and Statistical Manual of Mental Health Disorders (DSM-5), the focus for recovery is to apply talk therapy or pharmacological treatment (application of medication that is recommended by a psychiatrist, psychologist or family physician), the aim is to help ignite the hormones in the mind to return to normalcy and get you functioning at our best again. The nature of several of these pharmacological treatment approaches is designed to build up a wall that stops serotonin from impacting any other neuron and keeps the messages going from serotonin to serotonin, it gives it more direction and keeps the messages in sync.

I would like to engage in another form of connection that is clothed in a psychospiritual coat by asking a question about faith. What is faith? This is a subject that not many individuals engage in because it seems to spirit based or non-sensical for many in our community, so the subject is slighted or erased from vocabulary altogether. In a practical sense, it is a demonstration of faith when you get on your phone and open a skip the dishes app and order food from your favorite restaurant with the expectation that it is going hit that spot, you will not get sick, and you will not die. This is a demonstration of faith because you do not know the cook or the owner, but you know the name of the food chain and you strongly believe that this is good stuff, so you order and eat no questions asked. Accompanied by this faith is another player called to trust that you do every day when you get up get dressed sit at the table to eat breakfast, drive in your car to work or board a flight to go to another city, or just go to your home office to start your day. If any of these things fail to produce the expected results you get stressed. Now let us consider where this conversation began, it began by talking about faith and now, you are at the opposite end talking about stress, and these two trusts were mentioned. Let us analyze the scenario from above to see if there is any connection between psychology and spirituality. As a human being the need for comfort, relaxation and a stress-free environment is something that you crave like the root of a dry plant that is thirsty for water. Therefore, when it does not happen according to your ideal expectation, you get overwhelmed, and the psychological impact is far-reaching.

Here is another example of faith in action that you give whatever name you feel most comfortable with. You commit your life to another hoping that the individual will fulfill all your needs. Therefore, we go all in, and sometimes after just a short time of getting to know them you move in with the person, make big financial decisions, have children, and get married. Maybe this is not faith it's bravery or being in love or maybe you are following your gut feeling that this is your soul mate it's all of this but not "faith." Notice by the way that when you are in the honeymoon phase of these relationships how happy you are? Happy is connected to dopamine levels in the brain and you feel "butterflies" all day long as she or he wows you off your feet and you float around on cloud nine. Here is another scenario to consider that is relatable to most people in the world. When you send out a resume and walk in the front door of an organization like a law firm, an engineering company, google, or amazon, or you just got hired as part of a team in the oil and gas industry every week you show up with the hope that at the end of the two-week cycle or month you will see a deposit in your account. Banks take your job letter and references as well as the famous credit report and give you a huge loan for a car and a house because of the faith that they have in the system. Here is something to consider could it be that the world is more dependent on faith than we are willing to acknowledge? What we do is replace it with words that are more acceptable in the professional realm. How ironic that cooperate America and the rest of the world function on faith but it has been revolutionized to be referred to as a business agreement, after all, how would it sound if they were to say I have faith that you are an asset and things will work out fine? That is not a very "professional" way to agree, a contract on the other hand gives individuals a sense of safety and has legal backing to address any ramifications that may arise.

Is it possible that the foundational principles that most fortune five hundred corporations are rooted in are a faith factor that dominates their decision-making? None of these guys have any guarantee that data collection and the previous track record guarantee inevitable success in the future it is all based on a measure of faith. This might not be acknowledged as a real element because there is no Richter scale to measure its intensity and no thermometer to determine how hot or cold it is. A person of some form of spiritual belief will recognize the possibility of faith and that it exists even if it's beyond their ability to comprehend it. On the other hand, if I have no form of spiritual belief faith is not a word, it is not considered more important than a cup of coffee or a couple of dollars in my pocket. Logic replaces faith and intellect appears to supersede anything too complicated. In the book called the Bible there is a text found in Hebrew 11:

> Now faith is the substance of things hoped for, the evidence of things not seen. Hebrew 11: 1 (MEV)

The definition above is based on the interpretation of faith from a Christian perspective. Faith is defined in the form of a noun as complete trust and confidence in someone or something. In the political world, entire populations base their future on faith in a political party to fulfill the mandate and improve economic situations. Someone might say that is not faith, but statistics based on the track record of the party and the credibility of the party members. This is a very practical way to explain it in the field of political science or media analysis, but it still does not rule out the fact that there is some measure of faith demonstrated when we show up to vote. The psychology is that this individual will fulfill your expectations and help to ease the population's concerns for a better quality of life. Could it be that this is faith? Now I would like to continue to solicit your engagement in this conversation about faith. Is it a real force in the universe that only some people embrace while for others it's all about luck and destiny? look for example at the divorce rate. In the Guinness world book of records countries like the Maldives have the highest divorce rate worldwide while Canada stands at number 29. Maybe all these marriages ended because of mere coincidence and chemistry that ran out too soon. Another definition of faith is confidence in something or someone.

In another realm, we want to talk about how faith is put into practice in the field of medicine. Many physicians are readily open to having the conversation about the reality that after they perform any form of medical procedure, they believe that based on their research and previous procedures that were successful the results should be the same. Outside of that what else do they have to determine the success of the surgery? Faith! They can deny the reality of the process but outside of their role and the medications that they can give for pain relief that offers physiological and, psychological support they give it to you with the faith that it will get the job done and the final phase will be successful. Plumbers, engineers, politicians, entrepreneurs, farmers, masons, architects, pilots, meteorologists, and every other known profession all utilize faith directly and indirectly, but the challenge is how many of these individuals will admit that this is true. Just recently we saw a huge catastrophe with the collapse of an apartment building that claimed the lives of many individuals because it collapsed. Those who were involved in the construction had faith in the durability of the building materials and that they will withstand the test of time. The building inspectors as they did their inspections had faith that everything was okay and probably did not see it coming or they did but were in denial. Who knows? What I am trying to say is not that the men were negligent but that according to their knowledge and expertise they had faith that nothing of this magnitude would ever happen. So many different stories around the world about incidents that occurred worldwide that has been called a disaster or accident. The next time you decide to visit an attraction around the world and decide to walk on a glass surface that is going across a ravine that is hundreds of feet in the air ask yourself this question, what guarantee do I have that this structure will remain sturdy when I get to the other side? You do these things because you trust that proper engineering protocols were followed, and you trust that it is so and go out on "the limb" and trust that nothing will go wrong. If you have the least bit of doubt that it is not safe or if someone tries to encourage you to take the trip, you go into a panic and get defensive at just the thought of taking the journey. This is another example of two opposites working against each other one is faith and the other is fear. One of these attributes gets you going and pushes you to take risks and act sometimes without thinking, while the other will keep you isolated anxious, and timid to take the next step. You and I live within this realm of powerful unseen influence that is tied to our existence and challenges us every moment of every day of our lives to make a step into faith or fear the one we feed the most is the one that takes precedence and fuels our psychological emotional health.

"We must not take the importance of proper rest for granted "."

There is an innumerable amount of research evidence that speaks about the importance of rest for our psychological and physiological health. Unfortunately, in several places around the world, the work schedule has placed individuals like yourself in an unfriendly environment where you struggle to get adequate rest and it trickles down on all your relationships. I stumbled upon this quote as I did my research for this book, and it fits perfectly with the psychological, physiological, and spiritual benefits of sleep.

Sleep

Sleep is effective and efficient in the process of enhancing the thought process, organization of new information, and solidifying memory, leading to more creative thinking, clearing out harmful toxins, regulating your appetite, and keeps your body looking good (Liam, 2020).

Your quality of life is also intertwined with getting good sleep. When you get high-quality and efficient sleep it will help to improve memory, regulate the immune system, and coordinate neuroendocrine functions. On the flip side of this argument, it is reiterated that not getting enough sleep will increase your risk of cardiovascular diseases, poor mental health, cognitive impairment, and mortality (Fu et al., 2021). This seems like a reasonable conclusion based on the findings from this research so I would like to ask this question now I could, where did sleep come from? Did it exist before psychological research or is it an unexplained phenomenon? If sleep is so important and has so many benefits maybe it is a part of your natural design that was intended to help with the maintenance of good mental health. Could this mean that there is a connection between spirituality and psychology? Is sleep only a physiological activity or is it also psychological?

Rest is rejuvenating and restorative and makes your ability to fathom the collaboration of the spiritual and the physical. This collaboration works in sync to build an arsenal that understands that one of your first attempts to access spiritual transformation is to make rest a part of your daily routine. Rest must not only happen when we can, we must make time for it to happen. When the mind is not suffering from exhaustion and stressed out with life events it is more susceptible to engage in healthy balanced internal conversations, grasp spiritual lessons, and be more psychologically stable to withstand the pressures of life.

The Mind

The mind is easily captured by negative automatic thoughts. These thoughts do not need any invitation and have an intrusive nature that attacks our psychological and emotional foundations and disrupts the equilibrium. Developing an attitude that can withstand the influence of this negative way of thinking and living will require a lot of effort. You must be mindful of the internal dialogue that is dictated by negative thinking and make daily efforts to confront these negative thoughts by questioning their validity. The shift in the psychological outlook will be accomplished when you question and rewrite these scripts. Writing them down and looking at the other side of the original thought will help you to come up with additional options. You should ask practical questions like where is the proof? Is this a fact or opinion? The culmination of this is to balance psychological reprocessing with the spiritual belief that is rooted in faith and hope. The combination of spiritual and psychological awareness fuels the mindset and ignites an attitude that promotes spiritual fortification. If you do not have this spiritual awareness, you will miss out on the spiritual experience. You should aim to experience growth in your spiritual and psychological well-being. Your spiritual journey is not dependent on opinions, dictates, or personal dogmas. The search to know if there is a connection, or if an acknowledgment of the value of spirituality will help to promote healthier psychological sustenance is an individual decision. The caution here is to not be too ignorant about spirituality that the lessons that could be learned are missed. For example, many individuals are willing to go and try sky diving, white water rafting, binge drinking, drug use, one-night stands, psychic readings etcetera. Spirituality, on the other hand, is as the saying goes too complicated and time-consuming so we run in the opposite direction. The thought that I would allude to here is what is the worse thing that could happen to you if you open your mind to explore the foundations of true spirituality. Many individuals are cautious about talking about or exploring the essence of spirituality because for many it is perceived as a dogmatic form of dictatorial directives that are more doctrinal than scriptural. Those who are in positions of authority to give spiritual leadership and mentoring cannot amicably provide spiritual support if they are not openly allowing themselves to find the balance that is needed between the spiritual and psychological. If the emphasis is more to promote psychological wellness it is questionable and if it is promoting spiritual wellness outside of psychological wellness it becomes fictitious and frail.

Practicing kindness, humility, charity, and letting go of self-centered traits will enhance your mental health because it attracts the attention of dopamine, which is responsible for mood regulation, muscle movement, and the brain's pleasure and reward system. Serotonin regulates mood body temperature and appetite. This process is both spiritually centered and psychologically rewarding and helps to concretize spiritual growth. The desire to extend these characteristics to other individuals is not just innate but something that is generated from spiritual awareness that is a part of the human DNA. You and I were born with this trait. Therefore, when someone remarks that they are not spiritual it leaves room for an interesting conversation as it relates to who we are. This happens because of misrepresentation and or misunderstanding of what it means to be spiritual. Spirituality is grounded in your moral compass and even if you are not following the directives that are outlined in the biblical narrative, if you believe and observe the laws of the land, they have their origin in the book called the Bible. Here is an example of how much spirituality you are following without knowing that it is a spiritual act, not just a moral obligation. Let us look at the supporting evidence for this concept.

You shall not murder.
You shall not commit adultery.
You shall not steal.
You shall not bear false witness against your neighbor.
You shall not covet your neighbor's house. You shall not covet
your neighbor's wife, or his manservant or maidservant, or his ox
or donkey, or anything that belongs to your neighbor." (Exodus
20: 3-17)

Many individuals are struggling to understand spiritual awareness and what are the intricacies surrounding this topic. I would like to suggest that spirituality is accessible to every person and all of us are at different phases. Some people are very naive about spirituality, and others are at the initial stage and do not care to go further in the realm of spirituality. Some spiritual people will sometimes go to an extreme that is not attractive to those who do not practice any form of spirituality. Some have good balance and understand the process and can give positive feedback that will help to clear up psychological barriers and encourage spiritual interest that is not just a moral obligation. Another reason for saying it is wrapped up in your DNA is because you are aware when you do something that hurts the other person. The hurt comes in several forms like stealing, lying, cheating on your partner, and many other behaviors that spark awareness in you and cause you to carry a feeling of guilt. This happens within us because it is a violation of our moral standards that have been eroded. We will now look at other areas that are linked to your psychological and emotional well-being.

oorganizes new information.

Is it important for someone on a spiritual path to understand how to organize new information? What this has to do with spiritual growth and development may be one of the questions that surface. What does it take to organize new information? Spirituality is not a static or stagnant experience it is a dynamic process that continues to traverse the psychological pathways of your mind with new information. The content and main theme of spirituality are not an interpretation of the foundations that is attractive and wins over the minds of cynics and charismatic orators. The human mind is very susceptible to information, living in this era called the information age means you must be mindful about what you take in. Right now, you are reading this book and the concept of psychology being grounded in spirituality could be new or you may be resistant to this concept. But you owe it to yourself to reflect below the surface to see if this is rooted in facts or a philosophical idea that has nothing to do with psychology. The subject of spirituality has evolved for centuries and the emptiness of many persons in our society has

The mind needs rest to function effectively

opened the door for more vulnerability among those who are uncertain and searching for meaning in life. Let us say for argument's sake you are not psychologically well for example, and you are struggling with symptoms of anxiety, depression, trauma, grief, compulsive behaviors, or addictive tendencies such as alcohol and drug use. When your mind is captured by these symptomologies it is more challenging to grasp spiritual lessons in their most simplistic form. A mind that is free of substances and not overexerted by foreign objects will be more welcoming to spiritual development and nurturing.

In the study of psychology, your ability to recall a time when there was a crisis, what coping strategy you used, and how you overcame the event is important to know. This approach helps to bring back to memory the strengths that are often forgotten when life happens unexpectedly. This is helpful because it highlights the exceptions. In the realm of spirituality, the experience itself is significantly enhanced when you can recall promises that give deeper meaning to the observance of spirituality that is rooted in a higher power or God factor. Supporting evidence for this spiritual observation is highlighted in this Biblical narrative that reads as follows:

And surely, I am with you always, to the very end of the world."(Matthew 28: 20).

This statement is simple yet profound as it brings a balance between the spiritual certainty of the deity of spirituality and a psychological reassurance that helps to lessen the tendency for you to be anxious and live with uncertainty. Difficult and unforeseen circumstances push you to a fight, or flight mood and hypersensitivity dismantle spiritual psychological efficacy as you sink into ditches of doubt. When this hits home, and you are struggling to find your niche in the community the challenge is, does spirituality offer an option to resolve the psychological pain and fill in the blank that is created when life happens? The foundation of this promise is rooted in a spiritual understanding of a shift in your outlook if this is real or a myth.

Another biblical narrative that promotes spiritual psychological wellness is found in the book of Exodus chapter twenty and it reads as follows:

> *Remember to observe the Sabbath as a holy day. Six days a week are for your daily duties and your regular work, but the seventh day is a day of Sabbath rest before the Lord your God. On that day you are to do no work of any kind, nor shall your son, daughter, or slaves—whether men or women—or your cattle or your house guests. For in six days the Lord made the heaven, earth, and sea, and everything in them, and rested the seventh day; so, he blessed the Sabbath day and set it aside for rest. (Exodus 20: 8-11).*

The corporate world in the twenty-first century is structured for work to be ongoing and unending. Several fortune five hundred companies design things like shift work to keep the wheels turning seven days weekly and twenty-four hours daily. Having jobs that are physiologically and or mentally demanding will add to burnout that results in severe cases of mental and physiological ailments. As you reflect on the concept and content of this text it arrests your attention to examine your personal and

We should aim to take a day off once a week

professional situations and ask yourself, am I doing my best to maintain psychological wellness.? Now you are challenged to ask the question, is there more to achieving psychological wellness? What if psychological wellness is enveloped within the principles of spiritual wellness and these two are associates in the grand scheme of things that helps to sustain a balanced lifestyle? What is this Sabbath recommendation that human beings are told to remember? Your body is dependent on a twenty-four-hour cycle. Within this cycle, you are expected to sleep in the hours that are dark as much as you can and engage in working during the light hours you can separate these hours with the AM versus the PM time zones. This appeal however is saying that you should have a day off each week to rest, reflect and recuperate. For many who practice spirituality from a Jewish perspective this day of rest is significant, and it is observed with accuracy and pride. A closer look at this group of individuals sees more successful entrepreneurs and business leaders because they apply this principle in their community. In the grand scheme of things, this is not an attempt to say you will not be successful if you do not observe the Sabbath because you may be reading this book and doing well in your area of expertise, and you have never heard of this or have no interest in knowing. The appeal is to do your research try it for a month and then make an informed practical decision based on your own experience. The observation of this Sabbath according to the content will give psychological recharge and spiritual refreshing.

leads to more creative thinking.

"Creativity is the key that opens the door to unexpected opportunities." true potential"

Creativity is defined as the tendency to generate or recognize alternatives or possibilities that may be useful in solving problems (Franken, 2018).

Is creativity important for spiritual enhancement, Is the law of adaptability important for you as you continue life's journey? Mental health is not a myth that happened from a big bang that occurred in outer space. Mental health affects all of us in several different forms that are linked to our origins or life experiences. The repercussions of these events create solitary confined spaces deep within your psyche. To survive the world and the events you build up individual safe houses and become enslaved by those beliefs. You see these beliefs displayed in behaviors like internet addiction, gambling addiction, and porn. All these and others that might not be listed here interfere with your creative ability and derails the possibility of breaking away from the habit. The need for humanity to regain this creative expertise has evoked interest in seeking out resources that will bring this equilibrium back. This desire opens the door for psychiatric interventions and or talk therapy which is aimed at helping to rebuild confidence and get back to creative coping techniques. In your personal and professional relationships, the need for more effective problem-solving and the lack of creativity make the process more challenging. The recommendation here based on the research evidence is that getting sufficient rest is an asset that will help you to be better at solving problems. Rest helps to recharge the brain and ignites the executive functioning portion which leads to better results, lessening of stress, and quality of life.

Clears out harmful toxins.

"We do more harm to ourselves when we are storing up toxins within, prioritizing rest will help us to experience a literal brainwashing"

The body was designed to remove toxins naturally through your kidneys. This organ is the body's internal filtration system that eliminates waste and free radicals. The brain is another part of the bodies functioning that is designed to clean itself, but this does not happen effectively if you are not getting sufficient rest. The mind experiences what is called brainwashing when you get an adequate amount of rest nightly. By natural design, your body is re-energized and repairs itself from the inside out. If you are going to experience this brainwashing, there must be more effort to get an

The mind goes through brain washing. effectively

adequate amount of sleep nightly. When you deprive yourself of sleep your mind is not rested enough to make the most intelligent decisions. Your body by natural design depends on its process to get you in the right frame of mind as you go from one day to the next. If your mind is swimming in toxins it is harder to avoid what I call a psychological shipwreck.

Regulates our appetite.

"Attention to what we eat gives us more brainpower to engage in the daily confrontations of the enemy of souls."

It is your responsibility to be mindful of what you eat to maintain a healthy body. Paying attention to what you eat is valuable for your spiritual experience. It is through the appetite that you introduce several unhealthy choices that impacts your spiritual life. Bad eating habits result in deteriorating health which impacts your psychological health. They are all connected and you have to take responsibility for what goes into your mouth because it influences the mind. Learning to regulate your appetite means that you are not just putting regular fuel in your high-performance engines, but you are using the best quality that will give ultimate results. Not making the effort to get enough rest will make your lifestyle choices for dietary options less beneficial and will eventually come back to haunt you with complications. Being mindful about how you eat and what you eat is important for your psychological and spiritual health because of a symbiotic relationship that is shared by the observance of this practice.

When you eat well your body is sturdier, you look and feel better, and your confidence is higher than ever before. You will not be bugged down with doubt about your appearance, which will have a psychological impact on you. When you don't have this concern, you are more optimistic about life, and you want to interact with the community. When you do not eat well or get adequate rest, you are less confident, more anxious about the future, and spend time in self-doubt and isolation. I am not saying that eating right will solve all these problems, but it may be a good starting point. Many dieticians recommend balanced diets as one of the keys to living a happier life. Notice here another symbiotic dual of the physical impacting the psychological. Through the appetite, you nourish your blood, body, and mind. Attention to what you eat gives you more brainpower and sets you up for better psychological, physiological, and spiritual results.

Keeps the body looking good.

"Looking good takes a lot of work for most people but maybe we need to go back to the drawing board."

So, what does looking good have to do with psychological and spiritual wellness? A large percentage of individuals in your community struggle with self-esteem in many cases, it is rooted in personal body shaming beliefs of people who are not proud of their body parts and spend hours to match the requirements of societal "norms." Looking good is related to feeling good, and that is fueled by your internal perceptions of who you are. When your mind is in the right place, you are confident. This confidence boost adds value to the outlook of self, and how well you relate in a personal and professional setting. Exercise and eating according to the experts will help with self-improvement. Another critical aspect of external beauty that is noticeable is getting sufficient rest. There is a wave that is sweeping over our community. People from every culture, race, and ethnicity are looking for many options to look better. The psychology behind this is not a secret. When you look better, you feel better and hence your confidence goes up and you interact with more surety in all your daily activities. Sometimes the real answer lies in getting an adequate amount of rest daily. Sometimes, you make huge sacrifices to get the job done, and in the end, you feel accomplished. And then, you work extra hard to improve your appearance by adding a little extra cosmetic or surgery to boost the appearance and feel satisfied that you are fit for public eyes. This could probably be a good time to look at how much rest you get each day.

When I was doing my undergrad, I had one colleague who

made it his sole purpose to get as much sleep as humanly possible even if we had plans to meet as a group to study, he had to get his sleep. We learned this on a particular day when we were trying to find this guy and he was missing in action in the middle of the day. A little later in the afternoon, we saw him looking like he was just coming from the spa well dressed, smelling good, looking good and we asked him, man, where were you? With no remorse or apology, he told us that he was getting some rest because he was behind in his sleep. We thought that was the most hilarious thing we ever heard because how do you catch up on sleep after it is gone? But over time, I have come to realize that even if you cannot regain sleep that is lost, it is valuable for you to make it a priority and be consistent. Looking good takes a lot of work for most people but maybe you need to go back to the drawing board and begin to take a more aggressive approach to make sure that rest is not optional on your agenda.

Efficient thought process

"We can become the master of our thoughts, or our thoughts can be our master."

You can become the master of your thoughts, or your thoughts can be your master." In psychology, one of the most popular known therapy approaches is cognitive-behavioral therapy (CDT). This treatment modality teaches how to reconstruct thoughts that are negatively influencing your emotional and psychological health. Therefore, psychologically speaking this technique helps to retrain your brain to think differently by capturing the thoughts that are overly intrusive and dictatorial that show up uninvited into your psyche and causes chaos to your functionality.

Let us look to see if cognitive behavioral therapy has any connection to or maybe has an affiliation or foundational principle that is spiritual. During my research to write this book, I discovered this verse in the Bible that I would like to highlight

"Finally, brothers, whatsoever things are true, whatsoever things

*are honest, whatsoever things are just, whatsoever things are pure, whatsoever things are lovely, whatsoever things are of good report; if there be any virtue, and if there be any praise, think on these things." **(Philippians 4: 8)***

According to the content of this verse, thoughts are very important in the spiritual realm, and according to the previous paragraph, thoughts are important in the psychological realm. Could it be then that there is a connection between the spiritual and psychological that happens by default? I would now like to engage your mind to reflect on a list of questions to see if you can identify the answers. What is the main catalyst that drives you to reach your goal or end up way off target? What makes you confident in your relationship and avoids co-dependency? What gets a child to engage in a task that was at first very challenging but then improved over time and became an expert? What fuels determination, commitment, and a winning attitude that drives you to the finish line? By now you might have guessed it, the answer to all these questions is your thoughts.

Psychological and spiritual are connected

I was privileged to interview Olympic champion Dr. Gregory Haughton on XY Spark a podcast that I host. During the interview, I asked Dr. Haughton about his preparation for these events and how he came out winning a medal with big-name athletes like Michael Johnson. His response to my question was an amazing example of how powerful thoughts can be as you visualize and construct a winning attitude. These were his words to me during the interview "Rolando before I run the race physically, I would sit and envision myself running that race a thousand times in my mind." His disclosure during this interview is a practical example of a psychological preparation sandwiched by a spiritual principle that gave him success. Why do I say it is spiritual? I say it is spiritual because according to the verse Dr, Haughton was reflecting on lovely things and of good report accompanied by hard work and determination.

Speaking from a psychological perspective the brain is an

amazing organ that needs to be fed with the right nutrients to produce positive results. You may be familiar with the terminology of garbage in garbage out. if your mind is not getting the proper attention it cannot withstand pressure. It is not realistic to expect yourself to do well under pressure if you are not taking the necessary steps. When you have some spiritual awareness coupled with psychological sustenance it is harder to be swamped with doubt and fear. The verse recorded above could be a gentle reminder about the value of practicing to get on top of your game by paying attention to the things that you think about every moment of your life. If you are pessimistic, frustrated more often than normal, mad at the world, isolated from reality, anxious about the future, and feel overwhelmed about the things in life that you have no control over, maybe it is because of the way you think. The final appeal from this section would be for you to look at the internal chapter or sentence that has been the foundation of your existence and begin to rewrite that script and start a new chapter as you dictate the events from now. Let this be your new pledge, "from now on I will be the master of my thoughts, I am no longer scared or ashamed of my past."

Open-up

"My unwillingness to admit that I am struggling and hiding from the reality about the impediments is causing interference in my growth" ".

In my role as a clinician, one of the most popular desires of my clients is to overcome an issue or work on their relationship or make a big carrier decision. A common thread that runs through all these scenarios is the need for growth and improve the feeling of accomplishment. As human beings we thrive on the values of personal growth and ever so often when you feel like this is not happening, you get impatient. In my last book giving myself permission to grow there was an emphasis to take personal responsibility for your actions and lifestyle choices if you expect positive results. This takes me to reiterate one of my favorite mantras "personal

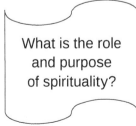

What is the role and purpose of spirituality?

development is not an event but a lifestyle." In the field of positive psychology researchers and scholars talk about the importance of spirituality. They reiterated that it is important for a deeper understanding of yourself and the improvement of life as you embark on this search for the meaning of the sacred (Peterson & Seligman, 2004). If you are fearful to embark on this search or journey to discover the significance of spirituality and how to apply it to yourself. Could you be denying yourself the opportunity to discover another facet that can help to improve your life? On the other hand, you can resist this quest and its existence, but it will not change the reality of the existence of things spiritual. So, then what is the role and purpose of spirituality? Several researcher psychologists agree that it is a positive state of mind that is universally acceptable and experienced by most people in the world (Lopez et al., 2019). As a psychotherapist, I would challenge anyone of my colleagues in the field to deny the reality of a superior being and the existence of a power that is outside of the realm of humanity. I would then ask that if there is no acknowledgment of spirituality then the practice and teaching of mindfulness should not be a treatment approach for those who struggle with mental health issues. Appreciation for the potency of spirituality and its connection to psychology is emphasized by scholars like (Pargament & Mahoney, 2017). In various places around the world people, recognize the existence of the sacred and how it has contributed to them living in a positive space and state of mind. They practice from day to day experiencing things like meditation, prayer, and the singing of or listening to spiritual songs through words being song or instrumental. Let us now look at some statistical facts from research psychologists who believe that spirituality is a "cultural fact "and approximately 95% of North Americans believe in the existence of God. Prayer is recognized as one of the mediums of communication with God. This is practiced by 86% and there is the belief that religion is an important part of well-being (Hoge, 1996). A special appeal has been made to psychologists and I would like to add that this should be noted by those aspiring psychologists. More attention should be given to the importance of spiritual dimensions in the members of our community (Hummer et al., 1999). The field of psychology has recommended that most of the inhabitants of the earth relate to some form of spirituality that is connected to their psychologist may not embrace this reality, but it does not negate that this is a fact. To deny this is to remain in ignorance and be less effective in treating the clients that are coming to you to find solutions to heal from psychological pain and spiritual insufficiency.

Every known individual practices some form of spirituality that is rooted in the acknowledgment of what is referred to in the research as the sacred or God. In Alcoholic Anonymous (AA) there is the acknowledgment of a higher power. This higher power gives those in recovery hope to know that there is a power outside of the self that can provide spiritual support. Right now, you may be asking what spiritual support is. Do I need to go to a priest or church? No, you just need to acknowledge that there is a higher power and access that through praying. In my practice as a psychotherapist, several individuals have verbally expressed how their lives have shifted and become more meaningful as they learn the art of balancing the psychological and the spiritual. There is a so-called research psychologist who argues that the connection between the two and how they collaborate to enhance positive life outcomes is not specific (Lopez et al., 2019). On the other hand, neither can be denied the research about how spirituality adds more value to individuals' mental and physical well-being (Cragun et al., 2016).

Psychology is defined as the study of mind and behavior. It seeks to explore biological influences, social pressures, and environmental factors that influence the way human beings think act, and feel (Cherry, 2020). Several arms of psychology are geared toward finding solutions to problems through the study of behaviors and mind-body connections. Cognitive psychology for example is the study of human thought processes, clinical psychology is the diagnosis and treatment of mental disorders, and personality psychology looks at how personality develops and the patterns of thoughts (Cherry, 2020). There seems to be a recurring decimal that all these different arms of psychology have in common and that is the study of thought and how to teach those we serve in the community how to retrain the brain and change the programming. Researchers who were more open to exploring the value of a spiritual experience and how it can heal the brain recommended that reading the Bible is good for healing the brain (Dookie, 2020). According to the author, anyone that engages in the process to practice biblical mediation will experience brain transformation.

> *"Finally, brethren, whatever things are true, whatever things are noble, whatever things are just, whatever things are pure, whatever things are lovely, whatever things are of good report, if there is any virtue and if there is anything praiseworthy— meditate on these things." (Philippians 4:8)*

The year 2020-21 has been unprecedented and surreal, all around us there has been more uncertainty, death, and hopelessness as we see massive job loss and an economic downturn that has left millions in a crisis mood. Every next sentence has the same main theme when will things be back to normal? The impact of this had left no stone unturned and billions of people are not seeing any light at the end of the tunnel or any change in the wind gust that is sweeping through the communities. The influence of this pandemic has left many grappling with uncertainty, pain, and terror coupled with anxiety and depression that have taken on new statistics since March 2020. It is amidst these current events that those who do not believe in the existence of a higher power in the universe who is faithful, just, and true. Reflecting on the promises of God that are written in the Bible could be a good place to begin your renewal of hope. What is an important caveat to this conversation is to ask yourself what do you have hope for right now.

Whatsoever things are true:

I want us to have a conversation now about anxiety. When you feel anxious what is the main thing that makes it stand out to the point where it leads you to panic? Is it a belief in something that you think is going to happen in the future? This belief seems so real that it cripples us psychologically and places us in a place of fear of the future. You cancel your plans and tell yourself that you are not going out because you have

> Focus on the truth to overcome anxiety symptoms.

this feeling that is based on what if. Can you relate to this story or anything similar? Now when you come to me, I work with you to look at this storyline to see if all the points in your story are lined up and beyond the shadow of a doubt it is inevitable that this is going to be "headline news". So, we work together to point out the facts or truth in your story to validate the symptoms of anxiety. Anxiety will not have full control over your psychological well-being if you confront it with the truth. In this scenario, the truth is that you do not have any evidence that supports your fear of the future. It is all rooted in the what-if or worst-case scenario that was manufactured in your mind. When you think about the truth and the facts and look at the evidence present your mind will override the anxiety symptoms, and over time you will regain control. Do you think it is a good idea to think about things that are true from now on when you feel anxious?

whatsoever things are noble

You should work to keep your mind in places where there are high moral principles and good personal qualities. If you have belief in a higher power, God you should work daily to keep a clear mindset as you live in this world. The choices you make, the entertainment you feed your minds on, the content of your conversations, and the places you go for fulfillment. These are all important for your psycho-spiritual health. To be carnal-minded is death, but to be spiritually-minded is life and peace. Spiritual growth is submerged in your willingness to follow this principle as much as is humanly possible.

Whatsoever things are just:

This portion of the text is telling you to be conscious in whatever role you play, whether it is political, religious, or community-based care you must be aware of biased behavior. It has become so prevalent that people have developed an immunity to these behaviors as if it were the right thing to do. Those who are in high places of authority are displaying unjust behaviors misrepresenting the titles that they wear and making the thing that once was correct appear to be erroneous and outdated. These behaviors are hitting the runways of our lives with a certain charisma that makes them attractive and appealing to many. Being just is not a collaborative decision but an inner conviction you must commit to maintaining even under extreme pressure. This is how you can cultivate the right mindset to remain just.

Whatsoever things are pure:

Purity is one of those assets that was mentioned as one of the major ingredients that will qualify you as an exceptional human being. In the book of Matthew chapter five humanity was invited to a feast with a supernatural being. At this banquet, the supernatural being served a meal that was not aimed at giving physical satisfaction but a lesson in spirituality. In verse number five of Matthew chapter 5, it says, "Blessed are the pure in heart…" In a metaphysical sense, the word pureness suggests freedom from anxiety, lust, resentment, and selfishness while in the context of the original Greek language the meaning itself denotes three separate elements of pureness which are all interconnected. Firstly, it speaks from the physical perspective whereby you are pruned by His spirit to bear fruits that are worthy of harvest. Secondly in a Levitical sense, you are clean and fit to offer up sacrifices. Finally, in an ethical sense, you are blameless and innocent and free from all falsehood. To aspire to live a life of purity must evoke an insatiable appetite in you as you seek to grasp genuine spiritual development.

Whatsoever things are lovely:

The year 2020 to 2021 has been one of if not the most unpredictable and challenging of all the years I have ever seen in my lifetime. I have heard about the time of the great depression and the genocide that happened in some countries and huge natural disasters that wiped out several thousand people around the globe, but never have I seen a time that is comparable to this time where everywhere you turned the cry was the same. The onslaught of the Coronavirus and the many victims that have been left in its path. The repercussions that those who are left behind will have to live with for the rest of their lives. The challenge of two classes of people on the planet, those who believe in the existence of God and those who do not. During this global pandemic, many have lost hope and faith, some are no longer sure if God exists. Do you think there is an important lesson in this text that could help to change the relationship that you have with negative thinking patterns? Therefore, whatsoever things are lovely, how do you see lovely amid death, destruction, and decay? How do you see loveliness amid isolation and hopelessness? When your mind is consumed with worry and your body is enslaved in depressive thoughts how will it be possible to see lovely things? When those closest to you are dying or they are battling for life in the intensive care unit how do you see lovely? You accept lovely when you can radically accept that things are out of your control, but you must keep focusing on the way forward. What is He trying to say to me right now could be turned in my direction and you will find hope. Your spiritual impetus will be lit with the aromatic influence of the reminder that focusing on his loveliness by nurturing a mindset of gratitude will transport you to "walk on water" and soar on the "wings of eagles".

Whatsoever things are of good report:

I would like you to take a moment now and engage your thoughts to explore things that are of good report. For example, you are reading this book and learning some new ideas about mind nurturing and the cultivation of your psycho-spiritual health. That is a good report what other things happened in your life this week that was a good report? Did you collect the keys to your house, brought a new car, started a new relationship, made a new friend, started a new carrier, or retired early? These are just a few things that could be categorized as a good report. This next verse needs no added scholarly enunciation or personal interpretation, it is quite clear, and the main topic is that you must focus on things that are of good report. Remember in my previous paragraph I spoke about gratitude? This is how you live your life by initiating a good report approach every day that will change your attitude and your approach to problem-solving and coping ahead. This report is not the opinion of a well-known economist or scientist or renowned social psychologist but from the one from whom all knowledge of these recognized world-famous figures receives their minute knowledge about their areas of expertise. The words written in the Bible are a good report. When you spend time allowing its influence to mold your emotional and psychological well-being, your spiritual knowledge will keep increasing, and your ability to cope ahead and overcome psychological tension will increase. The exposition of the text that was used to engage more mental awareness is to bring to the table the essence of spiritual balance. It is important to recognize that these traits are like spokes in the wheels of your spiritual experience that keep you on a steady rotation as you journey on this spiritual pathway. The terrain will sometimes become overwhelming with unexpected events, but you must remember that unfortunately, that is just the way life is. The text challenged you to focus on the things that are beautiful and point to the attributes of a creator who has your best interest at heart no matter how the situation looks.

Spiritual balance is like spokes in the wheels of our experience.

When you focus on what is true you do not get overwhelmed with anxiety because facts are rooted in truth. We you focus on what is honorable your mind will not be saturated with all the bad that is in the world because you will remember that despite that there are still good people out there. Focusing on what is fair in the world may be easier said than done but it does not mean that things have tipped so far north that everything is corrupted and hopeless. Finally, as you focus on what is pure your mind will experience a change from pessimistic thinking and be led into optimism that makes you feel lighter happier, and motivated to take on your daily responsibilities. This is an important balancing act that will be spiritually fulfilling in these times of uncertainty.

Let go!

"Historical grief and trauma, abuse, and misuse and all the underlining issues from our past and even those that are occurring right now in the present moment which has been anchors of denial and self-injury".

Holding on to grudges, being consumed with anger, and carrying feelings of resentment towards your spouse, parents, and siblings all add another layer of inner conflict. Families that are at odds with each other and are not making any efforts to be reconciled are fertile soil for discord. You are a member of a church and it has been several years now since you and the spiritual leader have been at odds. You might be reading this as someone who went to another church because you felt so violated. If you are a pastor that leads with partiality because of what was said or what you heard. Elders are aggressive dictators and self-appointed disciples whose job is to make sure the members of the church are following the principles of the bible. Ironically sometimes these principles are based on their interpretation. If you are in psychological, emotional, and spiritual pain because of something that happened to you in the church or because something did not happen the way you think it should. Maybe it is time for you to consider what you need to do to let that go so that you can heal and reclaim your life.

Another part of the puzzle that must not be ignored concerns historical grief and trauma, abuse, and misuse, and all the underlining issues from your past. What about the ones happening in your life at this very moment? Sometimes these are the psychological anchors that keep you in denial and self-sabotaging mindset. If you acknowledge belief in a higher power or God, it is not safe to think that you do not need psychological help because this could end up being catastrophic for your spiritual health. If you do not believe that there is a higher power that is fine too, but you need to ask yourself what you believe in and how it has helped you in the past. If you claim to have a spiritual mentor or belief and it is not influencing your life positively, is it working?

Sometimes the main thing that will turn you off from being open to a conversation about spirituality is those who have a wrong concept of what spirituality looks like. You may have or know of a spiritual leader who speaks about psychology like something out of a horror movie. This picture painted by these spiritual leaders has led several persons like yourself to be turned off from the concept of spirituality. So far however do you notice how connected they are? A man called David in the Bible relied heavily on another man named Nathan. Spirituality has its place but coupled with psychology it produces a positive life-changing result. We are also social creatures who need to connect with another social finite person to explore ways to overcome our issues in the physical and psychological realm.

The act of worship, singing spiritual songs, and getting engaged in programs designed by spiritual leaders are very helpful to enhance your spiritual growth. The question that must not be ignored is what you do need to let go of that requires psychotherapeutic intervention.

Several church members need psychotherapy.

Sometimes you look around you and you can see that there is a need for psychological support either for a friend, family member, or co-worker. In working closely with church leaders' pastors and elders in a spiritual context I have seen members bullied by pastors and elders who feel they have the right to dictate the way things should go and that if you step outside the line, you will pay the consequences. These men or women who display these aggressive behaviors take things personally or continue to be defensive, are hard to get along with, and have an unwelcoming unattractive demeanor because of low self-esteem. The church would be more effective and attractive if you have people who are making the effort to deal with their issues at a personal level. The thing that you and I do is to heal from the pain that is rooted in our emotional memory banks.

Culture plays an important role in how you relate to anything that is not following the status quo. Sometimes cultural norms and dogmas have placed in our minds that to get help outside our faith tradition is wrong. Several "spiritual parents" teach their children this theology and prefer to see them in psychological-emotional agony. Spiritual growth will be enhanced more successfully when these individuals have developed enough guts to break away from cultural norms. Sometimes cultural norms can become deterrents and it is your responsibility to get professional help. The guilt that comes with some of these practices in families can be heard in several conversations or comments. These usually come across as sarcastic or humorous from individuals in settings with those who are often naïve that this was a cry from a heart that is hurting. Hurting with guilt and living in ignorance because of misguided spiritual and abusive leadership.

Taking the bold step to get away from church leaders whom themselves are presenting a false leadership model because of their deficiencies is important. Many pastors are not trained or equipped to deal with these issues in their congregations. They are passionate about preaching every Sunday or Saturday to members who are suffering. These members need more than a sermon or a comforting expression at the end of the service when shaking hands at the door. If you are a spiritual leader a part of your responsibility is to direct those that you are leading to get help from a trained professional. Many of our churches are suffering spiritually not for want of good preaching, spiritual programs, rich lively singing, and youth programs. Many church members have experienced sexual abuse, emotional abuse, physical abuse, and severe abusive type relationship with parents and caregivers that has left them empty, depressed, and robbed of the last bit of self-esteem. They are now hanging on by a thread to what is left of their faith in a higher power but there is not enough acknowledgment of this. If you can relate to this story in any way it is not too late for you to break out of this cycle today and reach out to get help so that your psychological health can be restored and your spiritual health can be renewed.

Several years ago, I was privileged enough to sing in a choir with a group of some of the most talented young people I have ever seen. Many of these young people had no formal training in singing but when you placed a microphone in their hand and ask them to sing, you will be left with feelings of hope and optimism. I recall the choir doing the rendition of a song entitled "I just can't give up now" and there were two young ladies in our choir who did the lead vocals. The original singers were Mary and Mary but they had no advantage over these young ladies. The line of the song that stood out for me was "nobody told me the road would be easy, and I don't believe He (talking about God or their higher power) bought me this far to leave me." I relocated and learned later that these ladies were no longer practicing their faith as before and I wondered if it would be different if they had someone to work through whatever they were experiencing psychologically and emotionally.

If you are a pastor leading a congregation, you must speak to your leaders about balance and spiritual psychological sense. It is your responsibility to talk with your elders, deacons, choir leaders, and musicians about how inappropriate it is to let people think that if they seek psychological help, they are spiritually weak. If you are someone who believes that all you need to do if you are struggling psychologically is pray, I would like you to consider if getting help from a professional could add another layer to your recovery journey. I was sitting in a congregation one afternoon listening to a pastor speak so confidently to the congregation that they should not go to anyone for help but their pastor. What was interesting about that is this pastor has no psychology background whatsoever and, in my mind, I just said, wow. If you are a pastor reading this book and would like to help your congregants point them in the right direction. Spiritual development is an individual decision that everyone should take full responsibility for and do what is necessary to overcome the emotional and psychological scars so that there can be healing. I would therefore challenge leaders from every position in the church or organization to stop saying this to their congregations.

> Spiritual development is an individual choice.

It's time to permit yourself to grow and it must begin with you making the conscious decision to let go. I want to acknowledge those congregations where the leaders have counseling centers that are accessible for the members to go to and work on self-improvement through counseling and psychotherapy. I would also like to encourage you that if you are struggling with any type of mental health find a therapist that is a good fit. I know for most people the struggle is to find someone who is culturally aware and shares the same or similar spiritual beliefs. I want you to keep in mind that you are not looking for spiritual mentoring but psychological healing and there are thousands of professionals who have pledged to work with members of the community to reach their psychological goals. So, step out and go for it, it is your time to heal and let go of your past.

Evaluate

"There should be consistent internal self-reflection and assessment of what the barriers are that need to be demolished and be replaced."

In Collin's English dictionary, the word evaluate means looking at a person to make a judgment about how good or bad they are. In its additional forms, the word itself denotes personal assessment and appraisal of self (Collins, 2021). This is a very important aspect of your spiritual development because knowing what you need to grow is as important as having the desire to grow. There should be consistent internal self-reflection and assessment of what the barriers are that need to be demolished and replaced. In the new international version (NIV) David once again displayed the essence of self-evaluation which he said in *(Psalm 139: 23-24).*

> *"Search me, God, and know my heart, test me, and know my anxious thoughts. See if there is any offensive way in me, and lead me in the way everlasting."*

Let us now use this expression of David to apply to the present as we unpack the meaning of self-evaluation. Search me is a move that permits God or a higher power to guide you by making the connection in meditation and reflection on spiritual things. The request to search is a request of desperation as you acknowledge the urgency that is required to find the answer that exacerbates the issues. The patriarch recognized that something was not right and that there was a fault in the system that needed to be assessed by the manufacturer, so he went to God or his higher power with a humble plea and an invitation to enter within. This was a move of humility and subjection to the process that is risky, transformative, healthy, and spiritually therapeutic.

I would now like to talk about David's confession where he asked his higher power to test him and know his anxious thoughts. Looking at this through a therapeutic lens makes it crystal clear, David wrestled with anxiety and recognized that he needed help, so he reached out to God to get help before he self-destructs. Anxiety is a mental health disorder experienced by every human being at some time in their lives. This can occur if you have a job interview, expect to have a meeting with the boss, expect a newborn, go on a long trip for the first time, have an important speaking appointment etcetera. This is just one such diagnosis that affects your psychological health, and it gets more intense when it explodes into generalized anxiety and or social anxiety. This may come in the form of panic attacks and phobias about the important task that you need to complete daily, for some persons they would be mentally disabled. When you are struggling with these types of symptoms, and please note this is just one mental health disorder, you have individuals who are struggling with depression, personality disorders, bipolar tendencies, addiction-related disorders, grief, and trauma, and some have a combination of these issues. It is your responsibility to acknowledge this and get help. Sometimes you may not see it but if there are people around you that you trust their opinion is valid, and they point this out to you go get help.

Mental health is not a myth, neither is it something to ignore, and remaining in ignorance is not a safe place to be. There is no human being on the planet that is safe from its impact. Your prestige, position, or pride is not a safeguard against cognitive dissonance and spiritual degeneration. As you reflect on your present state of mind and your present temperament you must be honest with yourself. When you go through this process do your research get on the internet, check counseling websites, do a google search, and set up a free consultation with the counselor to get a feel of it. Make an appointment with whomever you feel most comfortable with and get this process going. Depending on where you are at with your mental health need you may need more time in therapy, or you may need to connect with a psychiatrist to get pharmacological treatment (medication). Remember it is

You may need more time in talk therapy or medication.

better to know what's going on and begin the process than to deny the existence and it escalates and worsens to the point of destroying important relationships in your life. You have needs as a human being, these needs are necessary for your well-being and effective functioning. The table outlined below seeks to give a visual of those needs that are a part of what every individual craves in their daily lives.

Table 2. Hierarchy of human needs

(Complied in part from Maslow, 1962; Miller, 1981; Weil, 1973; Glasser, 1985; Whitfield, 1987).

---

1. Survival
2. Safety
3. Being real
4. Acceptance
   Others are aware of, take seriously and admire the real you.
   Freedom to be the real you.
   Tolerance of your feelings
   Validation
   Respect
   Belonging and love
5. Support
6. Loyalty and trust
7. Freedom
8. Nurturing
9. Unconditional love (including connection with a higher power)

Know what the rationale is for seeking psychotherapeutic intervention and then make the initial contact.

If you are reading this paperback and feel impressed to seek professional help do your research, look at the person's profile, and area of expertise, and know what the rationale is for seeking psychotherapeutic intervention. After this make the initial contact via phone or video call to get a general feeling and know if the connection is there. Because of the delicate nature of therapy, it must be properly evaluated, and then you can make an informed decision before you proceed. It is also important that you do not feel indebted to ask your pastor, priest, or spiritual leader for their blessing because if they do not believe in the process of therapy or do not understand the dynamic, they will do everything to discourage you. For example, you want to watch out for those who when you try to explain to them what you are experiencing is quick to tell you I will pray for you. After the prayer what next? It is reiterated by many leaders that faith without works is dead so you must follow up with works and get connected with a mental health professional if you want to recover from psychological pain. On the other hand, being spiritual may not be an issue that you have. You may be more spiritual than the meaning of the word, but you are emotionally, and psychologically malnourished, and personal evaluation will ignite brutal honesty. It is time for more spiritually minded people to give themselves permission to grow spiritually and look within to see the flaw and then reach up without getting repaired.

maintenance

The need to properly maintain the profession of your faith is important if you are going to develop sustenance and heal from emotional and psychological pain.

After you have experienced the process of transformation you need to formulate a maintenance strategy. Let me give you an example here by using an analogy. When you have a car to keep it running well you would pay attention to the oil change schedule, check the brakes, depending on the seasons and the geographical location make sure there are good tires on it, and so on. This is what you would do to maintain the vehicle for your safety and those are fellow motorists. Now I would like you to think about what tools you are going to need to maintain your mental well-being. This means getting down to business and writing out a strategy that you would hold yourself accountable for carrying out consistently. This process is said to be a shift from whom you were to become a new form of the previous, like a reboot. This is like a restructuring, it is a shift from living your life to getting somewhere to live your life as an expression of your being (Whitfield, 2006). This statement from Whitfield is an appeal to live the best of ourselves every day of our lives. The need to properly maintain the profession of your faith is important if you are going to develop sustenance and overcome cognitive insecurities and spiritual voids. I would like to direct your attention to this text that I stumbled on while doing the research for this book. This writer made a statement that I find quite interesting. It is recorded in a little book in the Bible (Job 23: 12).

"I have not departed from the command of His lips; I have treasured the words of His mouth more than my daily bread."

If you are not a spiritual-minded individual and you are reading this book out of mere curiosity thank you for your interest in this epilogue. Also, if you kept reading it to get to the final chapter, I hope that you have found some nuggets in the previous paragraphs that make sense. I will just jump into it and say that if you would like to learn more about the connection between psychology and spirituality take some time to read for yourself in the Bible. I would recommend you begin in the book of Psalms. Please note that this is just a recommendation, but you can decide to start where you feel most comfortable like in the New Testament, or connect with a faith community or spiritual mentor to initiate the process.

There are some valuable considerations for this habit of maintenance to be concretized and lived out as you proceed on the path of life. If you accept the teaching of belief in a savior, a higher power, creator, God, or sovereign lord it is possible that you had an encounter that opened you up to the reality that spirituality and the existence of God are not a myth. When you exercise your faith, based on my personal experience it opens the door to seeing the world through a different lens. Several years ago, I was passionate about going to university. The first day I visited the campus of a

University I stood in a strategic location that overlooked a good portion of the campus and whispered a prayer in my heart with a special request to grant me access to pursue my dreams. I had no

Faith helps you see the world through a different lens.

money, no high school degree, and was not eligible for a student loan. The possibility looked hopeless and ridiculous. How will a man in his late 20s with no money, no support, and little to no educational qualification get into university? All the evidence was pointing to that which was most practical and realistic when you put all the pieces together. Forget it move on and as my dad would say with so much confidence "don't hang your hat where you cannot reach it." The ground beneath my feet was shaky and there was an undertone occurring like an earthquake as the foundation seemed like it was slipping away with no one to rescue my thoughts that this dream is not just a dream but a nightmare because the evidence was real. But then there was faith and friends who had faith to speak life into me and change my experience. Writing this portion of the book is very emotional for me to highlight that it was the faith of spiritual friends who saw in me what I did not see in myself.

Three young men are still my closest friends, we have been like brothers for the past 25 years and the support that they gave to me renewed my faith. Their support was not monetary because we all came from humble beginnings. The support was more valuable than cryptocurrency or gold, the support that was given came in the form of encouragement and counsel. These three young men (present-day Shadrach, Meshach, and Abednego) spoke words to me that were never spoken to me and never have been after that and it changed the landscape of my experience forever. Many people are spiritual, but not all have a connection or common sense that is not self-centered and egotistic. Research out of Harvard from social psychologist David McClelland said: "the people with whom we habitually associate are our "reference group" and they determine as much as 95% of our failures or success in life." Sometimes you struggle to accept or even open yourself to the possibility that spirituality is not harmful and useless because we are not lined up with the right people.

Maybe you are like me who was raised around people like my father who are sometimes very careful about stepping out of their comfort zone and they project that belief onto everyone that they encounter. The psychological impact of that is far-reaching and even detrimental to psychological wellness and personal growth. It was not until my late 20's that I realized that it was okay to hang my hat higher because it will challenge me to stretch up and look up to and give me new perspectives. Your mental health and wellness are your responsibility just as discovering your spiritual self is important for your well-being. Griffin and Tyrell captured the need for spirituality as a part of our well-being in their wheel of needs diagram as they talked about higher needs. In the map, they referred to the need for meaning, purpose, inspiration, peace, and a spiritual life of some kind. According to these guys, a spiritual life of some kind brings value to your life and is important for your well-being. Could this be your cue to pay more attention to the possibility that maybe it would not be as harmful as you first thought to go on that journey to discover what that would look like and use it as a part of your recovery from extreme mental and psychological instability? What if opening yourself up to go on this journey to connect with your spiritual self is what has been missing all your life? Are you ready to come out of your comfort zone and make that step?

I am spiritual and I am also a registered psychotherapist knowing both disciplines has added several layers to my approach as a professional because I can see beyond the surface of psychology and trust me the surface of psychology goes deep. What I am saying is that some psychological issues are also spiritual and knowing both has given me the tools to facilitate the right form of therapeutic dialogue with my clients. You might ask the question here, what is my agenda and why write this epilogue? I will gladly say that as a therapist my agenda is to engage with my clients and go with them on a journey of self-discovery and healing. Psychology works on changing thought patterns, overcoming negative self-thought, eliminating self-harming behaviors, and getting past psychological disorders. So far it has been working well and moving forward the recommendation is that the field of psychology would go even further if more professionals were open to the integration of more spiritual awareness in the approach to therapy. Just as how it is vital to not rule out culture it is also important to not overlook spirituality because the origin of psychology may be rooted in spirituality. I will close with this bible text that was used earlier that is found in Philippians 4: 8, finally, brothers and sisters whatever is true, whatever is noble, whatever is right, whatever is pure, whatever is lovely, whatever is admirable if anything is excellent or praiseworthy think on these things. Could this be one of the missing pieces that are needed to increase the healing and success in the field of psychology? Are psychology and spirituality connected in more ways than we are willing to accept? How do you think your life and well-being would improve if you engaged in this process of personal exploration? I hope that reading this book encouraged you to be open to the possibility that God, the creator, higher power invented psychology and you have no need to deny or resist the relationship between spirituality and psychology.

Contact information

Email: <u>hyman@xyspark.org</u>

<u>Tips4therapy@gmail.com</u>

Other published books

eBooks:

*Masculinity   <u>Reset-https://www.amazon.com/Healthy-masculinity-reset-Practical-solutions</u>
<u>-ebook/dp/B09HQ65KXZ/ref=sr_1_1?crid=3OR3G3WK3WG5J&keywords=masculinity+reset&</u>
<u>qid=1669219490&sprefix=masculinity+reset%2Caps%2C130&sr=8-1</u>*

Healthy Masculinity Renewed: https://www.amazon.com/Healthy-Masculinity-Renewed-self-esteem-masculinity-ebook/dp/B09MB7C6TZ/ref=sr_1_1?crid=3SZ841HP0EKR8&keywords=healthy+masculinity+renewed&qid=1669219683&sprefix=healthy+masculinity+renewed%2Caps%2C119&sr=8-1

Healthy Masculinity Reload: https://www.amazon.com/Healthy-Masculinity-Reload-development-masculinity-ebook/dp/B09MJN31ZW/ref=sr_1_1?crid=2XWBNGSJG55ML&keywords=healthy+masculinity+reload&qid=1669219759&sprefix=healthy+masculinity+reload%2Caps%2C116&sr=8-1

Instagram.com/xy.spark
Instagram: instagram.com/xystribe
Podcast: xyspark.podbean.com
Facebook: https://www.facebook.com/xyspark/
Phone: 1 (780) 659-1758

CPSIA information can be obtained
at www.ICGtesting.com
Printed in the USA
LVHW100811131222
735076LV00011B/332/J